"VOLUME THREE"

Part One: God the Father Speaks to His Children

Part Two: The Blessed Mother Speaks to Her Bishops, Priests and Religious

Direction for Our Times as given to "Anne,"
A Lay Apostle

October 11, 2004

Dear Friends,

I am very much impressed with the messages delivered by Anne who states that they are received from God the Father, Jesus, and the Blessed Mother. They provide material for excellent and substantial meditation for those to whom they are intended, namely to the laity, to bishops and priests; and sinners with particular difficulties. These messages should not be read hurriedly but reserved for a time when heartfelt recollection and examination can be made.

I am impressed by the complete dedication of Anne to the authority of the magisterium, to her local Bishop and especially to the Holy Father. She is a very loyal daughter of the Church.

Sincerely in Christ,

Philip M. Hannan

Archbishop Philip M. Hannan, (Ret.)
President of FOCUS Worldwide Network
Retired Archbishop of New Orleans

PMH/aac

"VOLUME THREE"

Direction for Our Times as given to "Anne,"
a Lay Apostle

ISBN#0-9766841-2-8

Publisher:
Direction for Our Times
12560 Holiday Drive
Alsip, IL 60803
1-708-385-7755
www.directionforourtimes.com

Manufactured in the United States of America

Graphic Design: Pete Massari

Table of Contents

Volume Three

Introduction

Dear Reader,

I am a wife, mother of six, and a Secular Franciscan.

At the age of 20, I was divorced for serious reasons and with pastoral support in this decision. In my mid 20s, I was a single parent, working and bringing up a daughter. As a daily mass communicant, I saw my faith as sustaining and had begun a journey toward unity with Jesus, through the Secular Franciscan Order or Third Order.

My sister travelled to Medjugorje and came home on fire with the Holy Spirit. After hearing of her beautiful pilgrimage, I experienced an even more profound conversion. During the following year, I experienced various levels of deepened prayer, including a dream of the Blessed Mother, where she asked me if I would work for Christ. During the dream she showed me that this special spiritual work would mean I would be separated from others in the world. She actually showed me my extended family and how I would be separated from them. I told her that I did not care. I would do anything asked of me.

Shortly after, I became sick with endometriosis. I have been sick ever since, with one thing or another. My sicknesses are always the types that mystify doctors in the beginning. This is part of the cross and I mention it because so many suffer in this way. I was told by my doctor that I would never conceive children. As a single parent, this did not concern me as I assumed it was God's will. Soon after, I met a wonderful man. My first marriage had been annulled and we married and conceived five children.

Spiritually speaking, I had many experiences that included what I now know to be interior locutions. These moments were beautiful and the words still stand out firmly in my heart, but I did not get excited because I was busy offering up illnesses and exhaustion. I took it as a matter of course that Jesus had to work hard to sustain me as He had given me a lot to handle. In looking back, I see that He was preparing me to do His work. My preparation period was long, difficult and not very exciting. From the outside, I think people thought, man, that woman has bad luck. From the inside, I saw that while my sufferings were painful and long lasting, my little family was growing in love, in size and in wisdom, in the sense that my husband and I certainly understood what was important and what was not important. Our continued crosses did that for us.

Various circumstances compelled my husband and me to move with our children far from my loved ones. I offered this up and must say it is the most difficult thing I have had to contend with. Living in exile brings many beautiful opportunities to align with Christ's will; however, you have to continually remind yourself that you are doing that. Otherwise you just feel sad. After several years in "exile," I finally got the inspiration to go to Medjugorje. It was actually a gift from my husband for my fortieth birthday. I had tried to go once before, but circumstances prevented the trip, and I understood it was not God's will. Finally, though, it was time and my eldest daughter and I found ourselves in front of St. James church. It was her second trip to Medjugorje.

I did not expect or consider that I would experience anything out of the ordinary. My daughter, who loved it on her first trip, made many jokes about people looking for miracles. She affectionately calls Medjugorje a carnival for religious people. She also says it is the happiest place on earth. This young woman initially went there as a rebellious 14 year old, who took the opportunity to travel abroad with her Aunt. She returned calm and respectful, prompting my husband to say we would send all our teenagers on pilgrimage.

At any rate, we had a beautiful five days. I experienced a spiritual healing on the mountain. My daughter rested and prayed. A quiet, but significant thing happened to me. During my communions, I spoke with Jesus conversationally. I thought this was beautiful, but it had happened before on occasion so I was not stunned or overcome. I remember telling others that communions in Medjugorje were powerful. I came home, deeply grateful to Our Lady for bringing us there.

The conversations continued all that winter. At some time in the six months that followed our trip, the conversations leaked into my life and came at odd times throughout the day. Jesus began to direct me with decision and I found it more and more difficult to refuse when He asked me to do this or that. I told no one.

During this time, I also began to experience direction from the Blessed Mother. Their voices are not hard to distinguish. I do not hear them in an auditory way, but in my soul or mind. By this time I knew that something remarkable was occurring and Jesus was telling me that He had special work for me, over and above my primary vocation as wife and mother. He told me to write the messages down and that He would arrange to have them published and disseminated. Looking back, it took Him a long time to get me comfortable enough where I was willing to trust Him. I trust His voice now and will continue to do my best to serve Him, given my constant struggle with weaknesses, faults, and the pull of the world.

Please pray for me as I continue to try to serve Jesus. Please answer yes to Him because He so badly needs us and He is so kind. He will take you right into His heart if you let him. I am praying for you and am so grateful to God that He has given you these words. Anyone who knows Him, must fall in love with Him, such is His goodness. If you have been struggling, this is your answer. He is coming to you in a special way through these words and the graces that flow through them.

Please do not fall into the trap of thinking that He cannot possibly mean for you to reach high levels of holiness. As I say somewhere in my writings, the greatest sign of the times is Jesus having to make do with the likes of me as His secretary. I consider myself the B team, dear friends. Join me and together we will do our little bit for Him.

Message received from Jesus immediately following my writing of the above biographical information.

You see my child, that you and I have been together for a long time. I was working quietly in your life for years before you began this work. Anne, how I love you. You can look back through your life and see so many yes answers to Me. Does that not please you and make you glad? You began to say yes to Me long before you experienced extraordinary graces. If you had not, My dearest, I could never have given you the graces or assigned this mission to you. Do you see how important it was that you got up every day, in your ordinary life, and said yes to your God, despite difficulty, temptation, and hardship? You could not see the big plan as I saw it. You had to rely on your faith. Anne, I tell you today, it is still that way. You cannot see My plan, which is bigger than your human mind can accept. Please continue to rely on your faith as it brings Me such glory. Look at how much I have been able to do with you, simply because you made a quiet and humble decision for Me. Make another quiet and humble decision on this day and every day, saying, I will serve God. Last night you served Me by bringing comfort to a soul in pain. You decided against yourself and for Me, through your service to him. There was gladness in heaven, Anne. You are mine. I am yours. Stay with Me, My child. Stay with Me.

Prayers to God, The Eternal Father

Dear God in Heaven, I pledge my allegiance to you. I give You my life, my work, and my heart. In turn, give me the grace of obeying Your every direction to the fullest possible extent.

God my Father help me to understand.

Part One:
God the Father
Speaks to His Children

December 17, 2003
God the Father

Greetings to you, little soul who seeks to do My will. I am with you and thank you for your beautiful prayers from the heart. It is My intention to speak with you and have you also record My words. Anne, I intend to give you messages for the world. All of this is My work. Jesus, who guides you so specifically and carefully, is united to My plan. It is this plan I intend to reveal to you in greater detail and from the unique perspective that only the Father of All Creation can share with His children. Anne, do not be afraid. When We are finished with these few words, I want you to describe My Voice for your brothers and sisters, so that they can come to know their God. What will you say? Listen to My Voice, little servant of heaven. Are you frightened of Me? Why do you want to cry? Is it because you fear My justice?

Me: *"No. I want to cry because His Voice, which is male, is so kind and loving. It does not sound persuasive, as Jesus sometimes does. It does not sound entreating or a little frustrated, as our Blessed Mother sometimes does. It sounds quiet and authoritative. You get the feeling that He has no questions if you know what*

3

I mean. All is clear to Him. He could be speaking at a million times higher level but stoops to speak our humble, limited language so this small, small, being, me, can understand. He is being careful not to frighten me. He is being careful to speak clearly so that I can record for Him. He has authority. There is no question. He carries it with no effort. It rolls off Him and into His words. It makes me cry because He is so good and I am not. Being confronted with this incredible source of love and goodness, I wish so badly that I was better, more worthy, that I brought more to this table of the divine. Oh my dear brothers and sisters, I've just gotten a taste of what it is going to feel like when we die and meet God. It's going to break our hearts if we have nothing to offer this wonderful, sweet, kind Father. Do not delay. Serve now, at this moment, in this day. The tears stream down my face as He is not a God of justice at this moment, but a God of love. This is how He is looking at you this moment, as you read this. Serve now. Delay no longer. Please believe that you will only be eternally grateful for anything you do for this God of Love."

God the Father: **"Anne, My creature, whom I created to serve, do not cry. You have characterized Me accurately in a few words. How many can say that? Be consoled that if you do nothing else for Me while you live, you have done that. You** *must stop crying now for a moment while We work and then I will comfort you.*

"Anne, every soul was created to serve in My Kingdom. Each has glorious qualities that will flourish when they follow Me. Souls think they have little to offer. That is because they are not doing My will, but their own. When they ask Me for guidance, they will get it. I will guide the soul to their rightful role in My Kingdom and their gifts will explode into development under My watchful and guiding eye. Souls feel undernourished spiritually. They are actually starving, My little one, and that is because they do not come to Me for nourishment. They seek worldly nourishment which leaves them terribly unwell because they think they should be fed and wonder why the hunger pangs continue. They hunger for Me. Well, as I have been from the beginning of time, I am here. I am here, dear little children. Your God loves you with a love that will set you to sobbing in joy, as this little soul has done. Do not fear Me. You need only fear Me if you are My enemy. And if you are My enemy, you will lose everything. So do not be My enemy. You were created to be My friend and to have everything that I have to offer. In the days to come, We will discuss what it is I offer you, My children. Your inheritance is too glorious to deal

with in a few pages. It will take time. But My little recording soul has graciously agreed to allow Me to write through her so We will proceed. This work is My Christmas gift to your world. You see that your God participates in all on earth. In this season of giving, I also give. Be at peace now, little souls of the world. I am here."

December 18, 2003
God the Father

It is I, the Father of All, who speaks to this small soul. I wish to give My children both notice and direction. If you are following Me, continue to follow Me, but in a more dedicated fashion. Ask yourself on this day, what can I do for My Father in heaven? I will put the answer in your heart, little souls, and you will have My request. Then you must step out in faith and complete the task I have asked of you. Through this first step, you will discover how I am going to work through you. Ask Me for direction, and in an enhanced way, you will be directed.

For those souls who are not following Me, but who understand that they must change, begin by prayer. Pray the Lord's Prayer, as given to you by My son. Pray this prayer often because through it you are acknowledging My dominion over this world. You are giving Me the praise that justly belongs to Me. This, little soul, is an act of humility and a good first step. Do this now and your God will stoop down to you and collect you. Do not be afraid. I am not to be feared at this time. Pray this prayer and all will be well.

Souls who are working against Me, I speak to you now with the greatest of gravity. You know who you are and you understand that you have pitted yourself against all that is Light. You must cease now. The time is quickly approaching when you will be compelled to abandon all hope. Read the words of My Son in this series of revelations. He wants to rescue you. I have willed it. I have willed that you, in all your sinfulness, should repent and join Me in heaven forever. You see, dear little sinner, I love you. Sinners with far blacker souls than yourself have repented, been washed clean, and reside here in heaven with the greatest of saints. That is what I want for you. You will not be reproached. You will be loved and it will be difficult for you to accept this love but it will cleanse you. You are Mine, like it or not. Come back to Me. Do not reject Me this time as I seek your salvation. Your pain is My personal business and I will eradicate it. That is My promise to you.

Souls, who have waited for this time, your wait is nearly over. You have struggled valiantly. Continue to do so for the moment, knowing that your God is grateful. How happy you will be that you served heaven while you remained on earth. I cannot reveal all of heaven's secrets because your humanity would not withstand such knowledge and truly, you would insist on coming home immediately. But I would reveal some of the joys that await you. It is My will to do this because in this time, souls on earth doubt the very existence of heaven. This spiritual starvation has left many without hope, so in response, I have willed that Jesus, Mary, his mother, and many saints, give you both guidance and heavenly information. I, Myself, am speaking to you now to give you the path or map to these times. I will not leave souls abandoned in such darkness. I have always provided My children in earthly exile with prophets and I do so now, in many areas of the world. You must see with your eyes, dear souls. Do not turn away from My heavenly direction as through it I give the extra help that many need. If you are called upon to assist with the spreading of these words, do so in all joy. Your reward will not disappoint you.

December 19, 2003
God the Father

My little ones feel great joy in communicating with Me. That is the smallest foretaste of heaven. In heaven, you will have instant and constant communication with Me. We will take such joy in each other, dear children. There is a complete absence of want in heaven. You will search in vain for the poor, the troubled, and the sick. Everywhere you look you will view another tableau of peace and serenity. Souls will seek knowledge and find it. Souls will seek wisdom and obtain it. Souls will seek understanding from others and others will instantly understand them. Such sympathetic listening will take place in heaven, My children. You will know nothing of anxiety for loved ones in heaven because all will be well and all will be decided. There will be no uncertainty in the hearts of My children. Dear ones, this is your destiny. This is your inheritance for which you were created. Your time on earth is a small capsule of time designed to give you the opportunity to obtain your place in heaven. Use the gifts I have given you and you will find no limit to what you can achieve on earth. All heavenly help is

*available. But we cannot see it, reply My
children in their poor little hearts. Dear
children, as you have been told, you cannot see the wind, but you see the power of
the wind and you see the beautiful things
that can be achieved when you harness
that power. I am the same. How does one
harness God? Simply by praying. As you
are My servants, I am also your servant,
in the sense that a Father wants all for
His children and gives all to His children. If a child continually refuses a gift
from His Father, the Father knows to stop
forcing the gift on that child. The wise
father knows that the child cannot be
given the gift until the child is ready to
see the value of the gift and accept it.
This may not be the father's wish. The
father wishes to give the child every gift
available and every gift that is valuable
to that child. But the wise father waits
for the opportunity to direct the child and
that opportunity comes when the child
begins to listen. Listen to Me, children. I
have many graces to give you that you
require for your salvation. How sad for
Me that My graces are refused and
rejected as though they are worthless. I
created your world for your pleasure and
edification. I did not create your world so
that you could sin against each other and
sin against Me. Look carefully into your*

life now. Say to Me, God, My Father, help me to understand. I will not refuse this prayer, dearest child, destined to be held against My heart. I will not refuse you. I will help you to understand exactly what keeps you from Me. And together, with all of the assistance of heaven, We will bring you to your rightful place. My courage is boundless and I give you a share of that courage. The world will pass away, dear ones, but you will be with Me.

December 19, 2003
God the Father

My children, as your Father, I retain a certain amount of authority over you. It is good when you acknowledge this and bow before Me. I do not want souls to bow before Me because they have been forced. I prefer My children to serve Me from motives of love and loyalty. Loyalty to God is something that has fallen by the way-side in your world. I gaze upon My creatures, looking for faces that look up to Me in love, and I find so few in this time. Many of you have been caught up in the noise of your current world. I do not speak of the natural noises of wind through trees, water from streams, lakes, and oceans, and the noises of animals as they serve their God in all their busyness. I speak of the artificial noise that you surround yourself with, in an effort to feel safe. Sit in silence, please. Remove this clamour from your life. I say this with all authority and understanding of the needs of the creatures I have created. Your spirits suffocate under the attack of all of this noise. In silence comes peace, the peace within which I would speak to you. Dearest little ones, destined for heaven, you will not know how to conduct yourself in the next world with its beautiful quiet. There will be sound in heaven, but beautiful, organized sounds, destined to bring joy to the spirits of My little ones. How you will weep for joy at the sound of the angels as they combine their voices to praise Me and entertain the saints. And you will all be saints, dear ones, if you listen to My Voice within you. There are also the beautiful sounds of My creation. Children, if there is a sound that gives you joy, you will experience it in heaven in the most profound way that you can imagine. Indeed, you can not imagine it, but you can dream about it and every so often I will give you a sample of heavenly sound in your life. Watch for these little experiences, children. You will find them on your earth. Because of your limited vision, which is My will for you at this time, you cannot experience heaven in its fullness. But your God often visits you with a portion of your inheritance. When you experience these things, look to Me in joy, and truly, you will find Me looking back at you in all love and tenderness. Thank Me for these gifts. They are intended to encourage you. Children, close your eyes for a moment. Open them. That is how quickly it will seem to you that you and I will meet. Your life is but a blink in time compared to eternity. Will you not give Me the smallest bit of credit? Look up to Me now and tell Me you love Me. Perhaps you are uncomfortable because you do not feel you know Me. I want you to remember that I know you, little one. I have always known you because I created you. I chose to send you to earth now. I had reasons for My choice of your birth time and those reasons still exist. So serve, little one. Serve. I will reveal Myself to you if you invite Me. Tell Me you would like to know Me better. I will not refuse such a request. You will become My intimate friend if you make such a prayer to Me with your heart. Even if you have the smallest interest in knowing Me, I will come to you. I love you. I see your soul in all its future beauty. You can not imagine what you are capable of doing for the heavenly kingdom if you will allow Me to work through you. In this time of peace, allow Me to put My love in your soul. You will not regret coming to know Me. Such a thing is not possible. You will only thank Me for coming to you. So do not delay, little child. Come to your Father, who wants only your happiness and welfare.

December 20, 2003
God the Father

My children of the world, look for Me. Look for the signs in your world that I am present. Some would have you believe that I am no longer actively directing the outcome of this time. Children, can you believe that I would lovingly lead My children for centuries, since the beginning of the world, and then leave? Would I really turn away from My precious creatures? This idea is fooling many souls today. They proceed in their lives as though I do not exist and as though there will be no reckoning for decisions against Me, against others, and at times, even against nature, as I created nature. I see all. I will judge every action. I will reward every decision made by one soul for the benefit of another. In the same way, I will challenge every decision made by one soul to the detriment of another. Children, all is being recorded. You will account for your life. I am merciful. I am merciful to a degree that will astound you. But you must allow Me to be merciful. You must accept My mercy. You cannot scorn My mercy, child. Allow Me to exercise My mercy in your life. How must we do that, Father, you ask. I will tell you. You must say this to Me:

19

"God, my Father in heaven, You are all mercy. You love me and see my every sin. God, I call on you now as the merciful Father. Forgive my every sin. Wash away the stains on my soul so that I may once again rest in complete innocence. I trust you, Father in heaven. I rely on You. I thank you. Amen."

I am acting as the merciful Father in these days, children. Pray this prayer to Me and I will respond in mercy. Your soul will be washed clean. Little children of My church on earth, you must not neglect the sacraments. Experience the sacramental graces of the confessional, and say this prayer. In this way the residue of sin will be removed from your souls painlessly. Trust My words, children. Do as your Father says. The wise one understands that a Father acts only in the best interest of His children. And so I act at this time.

December 20, 2003
God the Father

My children of the earth, remain in the awareness that I am with you. You should always know that God, your heavenly Father, is present. In every action, know that I am with you. In every joy and in every suffering, I am with you. I am not just watching, dear ones. I participate with you if I am allowed. To clarify, I live your life on earth intimately united with you if I am welcomed. What benefits does this union with God give you? You make holy and wise decisions. You treat other souls justly. You keep to the path that leads you to spiritual advancement. And most mercifully, for you, you serve the Kingdom of God and obtain eternal benefit for your soul. My presence in your life does not guarantee that you will not suffer. Suffering is part of your experience in exile. It means though, that you view suffering with clarity and wisdom. You view suffering as transient, understanding that it passes and you should be at peace with every earthly experience, even the experiences that cause you pain. Children, a reality that you should grasp is that suffering does not pull you away from Me. It can pull you closer if you are far from Me because it pulls you away from things of this world. I created this world for your joy, as I have told you. But the misuse of My gifts can confuse you and lead you away from your path to Me. It is then that I allow suffering for some souls. Do not be angry with Me when you suffer. Unite your suffering to the suffering of My Son and you will find that your ascent to holiness is swift and consoling. Children of God, children of the Light, you are Mine. All that occurs in your life has a heavenly purpose. If you do not see the purpose in what you are experiencing now, it is a good sign that you are far from Me and not in communication with Me. Come back to Me and I will explain all of these experiences for you. I want you to have faith, it is true. But I will reveal Myself to you in such a way as to help you to understand what I am attempting to do through you. I am a fair and just God. I will treat all with divine wisdom and mercy if I am asked.

December 21, 2003
God the Father

My children, you await union with Me, even though you do not realize this. There is always something lacking, something you are longing for, while you remain on earth. Those who are close to Me, and who attempt to serve Me in their daily lives, feel less of the emptiness. Those who are far from Me, particularly those who once knew Me and then moved away from Me, feel it to a greater degree. I do not care how you have tried to fill that emptiness in the past. What I am saying to you now is that I wish to fill the void you are experiencing. Souls close to Me, I refer to you too. I want to renew you. Souls far from Me, turn to Me, pray to Me, and I will fill you with such gladness that you will not regret your decision against the false gods the world uses to distract you. Souls undecided, I gently call out to you. Do you hear Me? Do you hear the Voice of your Creator within your soul? It is I. Have faith, little ones. I am calling out to you all. To some I call gently and quietly. To some I call with a thunderous command. What do I say? I say turn away from insulting your God. Turn away from sin. Come back to Me now, while I can salvage your earthly experience. Soon your time here will run out and you will have made your decision. Do you want Me? Truly, I want to be with you. I want to rejoice in you, My little one. I want to give you great joy, great peace, great security and safety. There is no substitute for the one true God and I am He. I have given you instruction on how to return to Me. My Son has explained how you fall away, how you stay away, and how you must eradicate habits that lead you away. Your heavenly mother, Mary, shows you nothing but love and care. She has brought many souls to heaven and will bring legions of them now in these times. Follow these lights. Follow these words. Follow this call and come to Goodness. Children, please, your Father wants each and every one of you. I want you to be with Me. I can say this no differently. When you turn to Me, I will give you a sample of My love. To many I have already done so. This is the very tip. This is the very beginning. I do not reprimand you. Because of the Sacrifice of My Son, your sins will be forgiven. They will be forgotten. I am issuing you a pardon from your sins, little ones. That is the kind of Father I am. I have a short memory, particularly for these current struggling souls who have contended with a time of great darkness. So there is noth-

ing left to consider except the love that I have for you. There is nothing standing in the way of you, My beloved child, and Me, your merciful Father.

December 21, 2003
God the Father

My children of Light, how filled with joy I will be when I welcome you home to your reward. It is always My will that you return to Me. Children, you will be struck by how comfortable you feel in heaven. You will feel as though you are in your true home for the first time. Once you follow Me and become My servant, you have an advanced awareness that the earth holds no true home for you. My servants must be prepared to serve in whatever place I call them. They must serve whatever people I require them to serve. My servants may be called at any time to do whatever the Kingdom requires. This is the way it is in a family. You are in My family. As members of the heavenly family, you are to be interested in the welfare of the other members, your brothers and sisters. Children of the Light, consider each and every soul on this earth your brother and sister. Your concern should be how to bring each soul on earth home to heaven with you. This is far too big, Father, you say. Well, dear little one, that is My goal. And because it is My goal, it must be your goal. A good child, an obedient child, always looks out for the inter-

ests of his Father. And that is what My servants must do. Now instead of finding this a frightening, overwhelming task, I want you to say, this task will be an easy thing, because My Father will do all of the work. All I need do is rise each day with a spirit of willingness. If I do that, My Father, along with the Son, and the Holy Spirit, and all of the inhabitants of heaven, will work through me in a miraculous way and souls will be saved. A word here, a smile there, a kindness there, an act of humility when pride would be tempting, these small acts bring souls back to the family and I can then bring them to heaven. My dearest little ones, your Father is calling out to you in hope and in love. Hear My Voice on this day, this day when mercy is being extended to your world. The sacrifices of many of your brothers and sisters are what obtained this day of mercy when only justice was called for. I, your heavenly Creator, wish you to make the fullest possible use of this time of grace. Join Me now, join the saints, join the spirits of the just on earth, and Together, all united, We will bring the souls of many back to My heart before the time of upheaval.

December 21, 2003
God the Father

I wish to speak to My children about heaven. The coming of My Kingdom is the coming of heaven or the expansion of heaven to earth. This is part of My plan and this is what the future holds for My children. Can you see it, dear ones? True happiness can be found only in the union of a soul's will to the Divine. When your will is united to the Divine Will, there is no conflict, no struggle. Only a very few find such union on earth. The seeking of this union is the path to holiness that you follow in your obedience to My commandments. You are making decisions. You are moving forward along the road. You are making corrections. This is the process. At times in the history of mankind, most souls on earth were moving in the general direction of heaven. At this time, most souls are languishing along the way. Many are wasting their time on earth and are not coming in this direction at all. In this way, souls are lost. As a God of mercy, I send all manner of signs and warnings. In this time, however, most of My signs are being ignored. Such is the level of distraction, that My souls no sooner see a sign and experience My call, then they allow themselves to be distracted and pulled back into the world. Children, pay attention. You must focus on Me and on your path. You must be disciplined if you are to remain on the path to salvation. And believe Me when I say that all other roads lead nowhere. My children belong with each other, loving Me. Hear My call of love, now, while I can offer you a soft and gentle transition to holiness. There is coming a time, as you have been told, where the transition will only be possible with violence. It will be a shock to you if you do not respond now. Children, if you are not following My words, if you are not united with Me, if you do not acknowledge and respect My dominion over both you and your world, you are going to be uncomfortable and frightened. Your times are over. My time is coming. There will be gladness, it is true. It is what My children have prayed for. But change is difficult for those without a firm understanding and belief in the next world. If you were asked to hand your life to Me this day, and account for it fully, how would you feel? Would you feel calm? Would you feel confident that while you have made mistakes you have done your best and can offer Me a fair trade for your eternal reward? Could you even say, God, I have wasted much of My time here on earth but I see that you are the Creator and I bow before you? That is all that is necessary for your salvation, child, but you are going to wish that you had a small bit of something to give Me. You might give Me your years parenting your children. You might offer Me your service in your job or your obedience and respect for your parents. You might give Me your patience with sickness or depression. You might say, God, I have risen every day and tried not to be dishonest or hurtful to others, despite my pain and misery. To all of these things, and to nearly every life that holds dignity and some measure of effort to be honest, I will say, "Welcome. Well done. It is over now and you are safe and loved." I will hold you against Me and heal all of your wounds and pain. You will be lovingly prepared to enter into the Kingdom. Children, do not be afraid of leaving this world and entering the next. I will be there, waiting to receive each one of you.

December 22, 2003
God the Father

All children of this earth, hear My call. Your God communicates with you in all majesty. I will do anything to save a soul and I have great power. The only thing I cannot overturn is your free will. If a soul chooses darkness over Me, there is nothing I can do, for your free will is My gift to you and the Father will never take back a gift once given. It would be alien to the very nature of God. But you will return to Me. Return now, in your heart. I am speaking to you in this way because I want you to be in heaven with Me for your eternity. Is anything above this as a priority? Could there possibly be anything more important? No. There is nothing more important than this one simple thing, to gain heaven. Put aside all else right now. Sit with Me as I minister to your heart and prepare you to meet Me. I want only your salvation. I am sending the greatest graces through My words to you and as God I would have you back in My heart from this moment on. Will you remain with Me, dearest soul? Do not go away from Me again. You have sampled the world's offerings and you have been left unloved and in darkness. I offer you all that is light and good. I offer you safety and confidence. I will nourish you in times of hunger and console you in sadness. You need nothing, only Me. So there is no reason to languish. Your God has called you by name. Come to Me.

December 22, 2003
God the Father

My child, for so long I have watched you. In some deep area of your soul, you knew I was there with you. I choose to be more active in your life now. I choose to lead you more directly, if you will allow Me. I want My children to be united with Me, but also with each other. I require a legion of souls who are living in union with Me, their God, and who are responding to My directives. Children, along with My Son, and Mary, his mother, I am giving you every assurance of your welcome. You are being guided in an unprecedented fashion and this guidance will continue. We will shepherd you through all difficulties. Many souls think that they do not have to return to Me now because they will have time later. They procrastinate. Children, this is not what I want. This is not what I am asking of you. I say, Enough. Come to Me now. In order to enter heaven, you must accept Jesus, My Son. You know this. Do this now. Do I ask this of you so that I will have greater glory? Am I a selfish God who seeks My own comfort? Children, surely you know this is not the case. If your God is calling out to you, if your God is sending all manner of signs and warnings, you must assume and understand that your God is trying to spare you difficulty and upset. I want My children at peace. I want My children to be detached from the world, understanding that the heavenly kingdom is their home and their destination. If you are on a journey, a long journey, and suddenly you arrive at your destination, do you not celebrate? Of course you do, children. You do not say, no thank you, we do not wish to arrive at our goal, we prefer to continue travelling. The longer and more difficult the journey, the more relieved you feel at its end. Such celebration greets the end of a journey. Can you imagine, children, what celebrations will be waiting for you when you reach the end of your journey on earth and arrive home in Our Kingdom? You will not be disappointed. Your God, I, your Father, have prepared the most glorious banquet with everything that is beautiful in creation. Children, earthly delights are nothing in comparison. Do not cling to the things of this earth. You will leave them eventually. Your humanity dictates that your time on earth is finite. Dearest, the earth itself is finite. Only I am infinite. So if you are to choose Me eventually, choose Me now. If somewhere in your heart you recognize that I am your God and you are My creature, come to Me now. I want your soul to be preserved and protected.

December 22, 2003
God the Father

Children of the world, you are precious to Me. Each one of you was created with infinite forethought and love. Each one of your characteristics is an act of My mercy. My God, you may say, not all of My characteristics are loveable. I know that, My child. You have certain flaws to overcome. Do you think I love you less for them? Is not a favoured plaything often marked? Does it not bear the signs of a child's love and interest? Children, I love you in all of your imperfection. I love you with all of the scars and marks you carry as the result of your flaws and mistakes. They mean nothing to Me in the sense that I did not make you to be perfect. I made you to overcome your weaknesses, and, utilizing your free will, to choose Me. I made you to assist each other. I created you to adorn heaven and little one, I want you here with Me. There is a place I have prepared. It is for only you. You have a home here forever and I would have you prepare to complete your journey. Do I frighten you? I do not intend to frighten you and it is not to frighten that I come. On the contrary, dear ones, I come to explain to each of you that you are always one breath away from eternity. It is the same for each soul who has ever been on earth. From this moment to the next, your journey may be complete. I will decide. In times past, souls would remind themselves of this fact and use those thoughts to keep themselves detached from the world. Because of the many gifts and advances I have given and allowed, My children delude themselves into thinking I am passé and that My time has gone. Dear ones, have you ever heard of anything so absurd and arrogant? You may say, surely not, God. No soul breathing the air You have given us would think that way. And yet they do. If you are a soul who thinks you have no need for your divine Creator, pause for a moment. Stop breathing. I want you to realize that at any time, I can will this. Such is My power. Do not think you are independent of Me. If not for Me, you would cease to exist. I am God. I am omnipotent. My own know Me. You are My own and I want your allegiance.

December 22, 2003
God the Father

My children, I have called you. I have pleaded with you. I have explained to you why you must return to Me. You should come back to My heart and remain with Me now in the spirit of loyalty and love. If you have a difficult time and feel pulled by the world, know that this conflict is your portion. You are earning your heaven by your detachment from the earth. You are showing Me that you are trying to become worthy of heaven and that you are preparing yourself. Children, the smallest efforts on your part will be rewarded in a truly unprecedented manner. The children of the world have been led far astray at this time but I come now to bring them back. I do not judge you at this time. I love you. I come to you in all patience and understanding. Come to Me in the spirit of obedience and you will move swiftly on a straight path that leads directly to holiness. No fear now My children. I have only good intentions for you. Be at peace in everything. Your God will protect you and preserve you.

**Part Two:
The Blessed Mother
Speaks to Her Bishops,
Priests and Religious**

August 8, 2003
Blessed Mother

I want to give you a glimpse of your future. I hope to prepare you so that when the time for change comes, you will move smoothly into the new order. My children are aware that the world is changing. Worldly souls think that they are orchestrating these changes, but in reality, God is in charge. He is taking their evil intentions and using them to implement His own order. Holy souls need have no fear. The plans of the evil one will go nowhere. Be confident and fearless in the face of information that would cause you alarm. You must remember that God is in charge because God has always been in charge, God will always be in charge, and I, your mother, am telling you this now. My child, do not be afraid to give my words to your superiors in the church. You must remember that these are not your words or prophesies. You are not responsible for them and do not have to prove them. How could you? These words come from heaven and they are intended to give my children advance warning so that the children of the Light are spiritually prepared. All must play their part and you will see that many are receiving communications of this kind. Be brave. Be holy. Be ready to accept your assignments with faith. We are relying on chosen souls to bring a great many souls back to Christ before the time for the Miracle of Souls arrives.

August 9, 2003
Blessed Mother

I would talk about fear today. During the time of transition there will be great fear. This fear is the result of the lack of faith that has settled upon this world. Faithful souls need to be told that fear is not going to help the situation and it will make people respond in panic. What is necessary is calmness, a trust that can only be achieved through a daily prayer regime. It is the regime I wish to speak about today. People must be encouraged to attend daily mass. In this way they can pray both for their own safety, and for the swift coming of the Kingdom of God. Daily mass is one part of their plan for remaining recollected. Another part is prayer in the home. I believe the family rosary must be encouraged in every home. It is this daily rosary that binds and directs the family. I can protect a family that prays in this way. When a family does not pray, it becomes more difficult to see that they remain united and pointed toward heaven. Please, encourage this. I also want to say that the sacrament of Confession must be dusted off and reinstituted. I do not speak of group confession at this time. I have nothing to say about that except that each soul must meet with a priest, the representative of my Son, Jesus, in order for the sacramental graces to be obtained. This is necessary for each soul to be a receptacle of the vast amount of graces available to the world at this time and in the near future. If a soul has not received this sacramental grace, they will not feel the peace I intend to make available. The peace given will be a deep and consuming peace which will eradicate fear and place confidence and joy in each heart. Do you want this for your people? Then you must see that they begin my regime of prayer. Time will not go backward, but forward, and the plan has been committed to. I'm afraid we must enter the storm, my dear sons, but we do so together. In an extraordinary way, heaven is joined to earth and the souls dwelling in each existence will work as one to bring about the New Time. Our plan is perfect. My Son is poised to return. Spend your energy now on preparing His people.

August 10, 2003
Blessed Mother

My son, your mother wishes to speak to you today about forbearance. Many of my priest sons today are scattered and not at all focused on their priestly duties. Is it any wonder their flocks are haphazard in their spiritual duties? I want my priest sons to come back to Jesus. I am seeking a commitment from them to institute this new regime with discipline and enthusiasm. We must all be joined in our beliefs and the way we live our beliefs. Truly, we can no longer have one group observing certain rules and another group observing others. Dear child, this will never succeed. And in order to do what I must do with you, we have to change. I am trusting you to put these words where they must go in order to see that this happens. You will have all of the heavenly help you need and more besides. You must trust me. I do not hold you responsible for what others are doing but I do ask that you make clear that a change is expected and no longer will Christ tolerate blatant insubordination to the Holy Father that He has chosen and given the role of His Vicar on Earth. My son, please believe that the times are grave. I will soon be showing you just how grave are the times in which we are working. Be brave and practice forbearance while I reveal to you the nature of your role in the coming of God's Kingdom. How blessed you are to be chosen in this way. My plan is complete and through it I wish to lead many lost children back to my Son. One soul is precious and worth everything. How much more important then is a world full of lost souls who seek only truth. The Truth, which has been hidden from them, will shortly burst forth with all Its glory. Do we want souls unprepared? Of course not. We must be busy now about our heavenly work. Pray and my Son will reveal Himself to you as the Redeemer. I am with you and will support you during this, the preparation time.

August 10, 2003
Blessed Mother

My son, I ask of you great obedience at this time. Put aside tasks of lesser importance and spend your time on this project. You must ask yourself what is necessary to bring my plan to fruition. I will be with you and I will direct you. This work is what you have been prepared to do and is your primary job for the coming of God's Kingdom. Are you ready to serve Jesus? Are you ready to protect the souls I have placed under your care? This is the question that all holy priests must ask themselves at this time. This is why you were ordained as the inheritors of Christ's priesthood. Do not fall away now when it is critical that your loyalty be without question. Some will serve. Some will not. This has always been the way and I do not want energy spent upon those who choose the side of darkness. My children must be protected. You have been given a great deal of power because we have decided to work through you. Do not disappoint your mother who is relying so firmly upon you. Begin by praying the rosary daily. In this way I can prepare your heart for a complete surrender to both My Son and His plan. There will be no uncertainty. You will be directed on a path that is clearly lit, with all obstacles removed. Once you have begun this journey you will be filled with confidence and resolve. Sometimes, though, it is difficult to take the first few steps, which are steps that must be taken in faith. Do not be afraid. We will bring you along. Truly, you have great support in heaven, for your role in this is important. You may begin to rely on this help right now. Ask Us. We are waiting. We will not give you a task that is not suited to your level of holiness. Your holiness comes from Jesus and He will elevate that level as necessary for this mission. Be assured, my son, that your mother sees to every detail. Ask for peace and Our divine peace will descend upon you like so many gentle raindrops. I bless you, and thank you for your fidelity to this cause.

August 10, 2003
Blessed Mother

My son, I am with you. It is with a light heart that I send these words. This world, so in need of cleansing, is approaching the moment for which many have pleaded. We, in heaven, have watched the decline of mankind until we can watch no longer. Do you see, my son, how differently people think in this time? Do you see how differently my priests are forced to speak? You dare not speak of sin or evil, for fear the powers will fall down upon you in condemnation. My children of the Light bow their heads in shame often at their own goodness. They can only guide their own children with the greatest of difficulty because the schools are poisoned with a form of modernism that threatens their very souls. You can understand why your Saviour must act or risk losing an entire generation. You, yourself, have asked for God's grace for young people. I tell you now, God can no longer protect His children in this world and that is why this world must change. Be warned, the time of darkness is at its end. I want to work through you to set the example of the New Time. You will prepare your people and others will emulate you. Your people, following the well-lit path you will lay out before them, will experience the peace that only comes from heaven. In an extraordinary way, they will be granted peace. It will be notable, because there will be nothing to compare it with that is from this world. Others will pay heed and desire to have this faith and goodness for their people. This will not be a secret, of course. You will willingly and joyfully express your gratitude to the One who is granting these graces to the spiritually starved souls under your care. My son, let heaven guide you, support you, and direct you. Be docile under our tutelage. You will want for nothing and you will have others clamouring to assist and support you. I will show you the way. Fear nothing as all such spiritual renewals have begun this way. We are entering a New Time and while we do this with quiet determination, we do it swiftly. I bless you and extend the blessing of my Son to you.

August 11, 2003
Blessed Mother

My son, you feel a longing in your soul to be united to Jesus. It is through this mission that you will achieve the unity you desire. It is always through duty that one achieves unity and a current difficulty for many of my priest sons is that they do their own chosen duty, as opposed to the duty Jesus has selected and prepared for them. In this way, they neglect the duty that We need them to accomplish, and that they have been formed to accomplish. Important tasks are left undone and my sons wander further away from their priesthood and the unity with my Son that would sustain and define them. This is not working. We must start anew. A priest must be like Jesus in everything. First of all, and most importantly, a priest must complete the duties he has been chosen to complete. He will know what those duties are by being obedient to his superiors and through much prayerful consideration. Jesus sends help, my son. He does not ask you to follow in His divine footsteps and then turn away, busying Himself with other things while His beloved shepherds flounder. It is not Jesus who has failed here, my dear one. But we must focus on our future. Next, a priest must always be concerned that he is walking the most direct path to heaven. In this way he is leading many, many souls behind him. If a priest spends time on side roads or with diversions, many souls follow him that way and do not return to the heavenly path. This, my son, is a grave problem today. I fear for many of my dear priests because they will be held accountable for their errors and the impact their errors have had on souls. A priest is called to a higher, more direct path to holiness and this is what he must concern himself with, as opposed to a person in the world whose duty often keeps him in the world. This should never be the case with a priest. Yes, he is usually in the world, but he is to walk with Christ in the presence of all humanity. He carries a bright light that is Christ. If he is too concerned with the things of this world or with his own will for himself, he loses the light of Christ and people do not see the brightly lit path they should see by following a priest. Your heavenly mother wishes to give you the opportunity now for priests to follow Jesus again in a pronounced fashion. My son, you can not imagine the changes you will witness. Souls will tumble over themselves to be back on the heavenly path. Priests will thank God for their vocations because they will be ministering to souls who long for Jesus and who only want to serve. How sweet for my poor dejected sons, who have been so scorned in this world. Priests will return to their rightful place in the world and they will be worthy of that place. It is that which I seek now, my son, to restore worthiness to your fellow priests. Will you help your mother with this heavenly call? Are you ready to serve your

God and become another Christ in this world of darkness? You will help Jesus to restore the light. Pray with me, that Jesus fulfil His holy will through priests willing to serve and emulate Him.

August 11, 2003
Blessed Mother

My son, I wish to tell you about Our plan for you. You are to be the recipient of the graces necessary to implement this plan for priests. It is through you we wish to send information, instruction, and grace. For a time, We will communicate in this way. Later, We will communicate more directly. Be assured, dear one, that mistakes are not possible in this endeavour because it will be Our work and therefore divine. In the beginning, much groundwork must be laid. This will involve talking to a great many priests about commitment and renewal. You will want to assess whether or not certain men are willing to follow your direction in a dedicated fashion. We want follow through now and will not tolerate anything less than a full implementation of this plan. Let nothing remain undone if you feel We are asking you to do it. Such faith you are practicing but you are not alone and you will soon be apprised of others who are being asked to work in this way. Our plan is perfect. It cannot be improved upon. So remain focused on its simplicity and you will find your way easy. So easy, you will wonder. But it is to be this easy because of the vast amount of grace attached, grace that was not available at any other time in history. This life-saving grace is what is going to move this plan and persuade souls that this is

59

the only way for each of their lives at this time. Such relief and joy will be felt, my son, because my poor priests suffer silently. They suffer in isolation, even from each other, because none want to admit that they feel empty and directionless. Only the few who are relying on me, their heavenly mother, continue to experience the flow of grace. Again I say, this is because of the great darkness. My son, spend much time in prayer now. Limit conversation because you are being infused with both knowledge and love. The love in your heart will be from Christ and will steady you in such a way that your only course is Our course. How grateful We are for souls willing to serve. Have no fear. We are with you and all of heaven stands ready to assist with your mission."

August 11, 2003
Blessed Mother

I am concerned about the lack of follow through on the part of my priest sons. Too often, they are given direction from the Holy Father, and they listen, and intend to follow the instructions, but then do not. We must have a universal adherence to the guidance and directives of the Pope. Priests must agree to be led by this holy man. In fact, they do agree to be led by him when they are ordained. So now we must have a rededication to our Holy Father, whom I have chosen especially for this time in history. My dear son, the only way to proceed is in unity. But unity does not mean a compromise with the teachings of your holy mother, the church. Unity does not mean we adapt to the teachings of other churches, not led by my Son's chosen Vicar. On the contrary, unity means we set the standard and be firm in our conviction that Christ established this church and He will guide it and steer it through these decisive times. My son, there is really no battle left. Yes, the darkness remains, but only briefly. God has decreed that the time of the evil one is over. He will soon exert dominion over your earth. What is left to do is the work of salvation. We must do whatever is necessary to salvage souls from this spiritual waste land. Your part deals with the reassertion of the authority of the church. No more compromise. The rules are clear. There is no need and no benefit to extended discussion. And this is the course I want you to take. Loving firmness. All of God's children are welcome in heaven, assuming the correct posture of repentance, but that does not mean that we are going to do away with the church God decided would lead humanity. The church is nearly finished with her passion. A New Time is upon us now and the church will take her rightful place as the leader in this new Age of Obedience. You will help to make this happen. Be at peace and meditate on these words in the presence of Jesus, because it is there, in your soul, you will receive your instructions. I am asking you for a great effort at alignment of your will right now. You must be disciplined in this regard. See this with great joy, my son, and you will please your mother. Many are called but few are chosen and I tell you now, you are chosen for this work. Be at peace. Your mother blesses you and protects you while you organize your priorities.

August 12, 2003
Blessed Mother

My son, you must stand firmly with your mother during this time. It is for this you have been prepared. I am with you now in a special way and I will not leave you. You will need to remain recollected but that is easy for one who prays. I want to talk to you about salvation. There are many who do not even consider their salvation so they do not see sin as a threat. They often do not consider the idea of sin at all. There is a great deal of time spent on the consideration of why someone has committed a sin. These are diversions, my dear one. The evil one diverts attention from the sin itself and creates a dialogue where a dialogue is unnecessary. Each soul is to be held accountable for the sins he or she commits. That is quite simple. Certainly Jesus, as final judge, will take into account every factor that was involved in every sin, but the deed will stand alone and there will be no such dialogue at the time of judgement. You see, my dear one, this modern world is so unused to the truth that the truth is deemed too difficult for people. But once the truth is again spoken, people will recognize it for what it is and cling to it. I must tell you that sinners, even those committing the grossest of sins, will cast off their evil habits and return to the Son of Man with the greatest of remorse and joy. Many of our children are being convinced that sin is not sin. They are told that sin is a choice or decision they can make and that it has to do with culture or development. Any ridiculous notion is absorbed as truth while the ones who tell the Truth are scorned and flagellated as though they lie and try to inflict pain. We must concentrate on the fundamentals, my son. Salvation is not available for those who follow the path of darkness. They find themselves lured to the evil one and often they cannot or do not extricate themselves in time. We will take these souls back now with a courageous focus on the Truth. God, your heavenly Father, who is all goodness, has given me authority over this preparation time. It is with this authority I speak today and with this authority I intend to bring about the plan for the salvation for this world. You, my son, are to play a part in that plan.

August 12, 2003
Blessed Mother

I speak today to all priests and religious. You must re-examine your vocations. Look closely into your vocation and you will see the invitation that God extended to you to serve Him with the gift of your life. Now look closely at your life. Are you doing God's will? Or are you doing your own will? This is an important question, my child. Your salvation and crown in heaven depend upon the answer. Much is expected of you, yes. But not unfairly. You are given every grace and consideration to complete the missions We have entrusted to you. You must ask for these graces, it is true. But be assured, the graces you need are there for the asking. So please spend time today, and in the days to follow, examining your vocation and your life and make certain that one is guided by the other. I will help you. In fact, we will do this together, you and I. Spend time with me, your heavenly mother, and I will help you to understand if there is any area in your life that is not in keeping with the mission God has designed especially for you since the beginning of time. We will then make the necessary corrections, and I must tell you, little soul, consecrated to God, that you will be renewed. You will feel such a wash of joy and peace that you will begin to step with confidence and enthusiasm. Truly every holy duty will hold for you the greatest of consolations and unity to Christ will suffuse your soul. These are promises I am making to you. A mother never breaks her promise, my dear one. Be humble, in doing this. Do not think you must prove anything to me because I know everything. I cannot be fooled and if you are fooling yourself, I will help you to uncover that deception and toss away the cobwebs that have hidden your duty from you. Truly, we will seek out the truth together and together, we will find the truth and set matters right with you. Do not be afraid of this process, my dear one, because if you let fear stop you, you will face this again, only perhaps not in such a sympathetic environment. A mother is all forgiving and obtains all manner of pardon for her repentant children. But even a mother cannot interfere with divine justice once it has been set in motion. So let us step with courage into the room of your vocation and make certain that all is where it should be. Be joyful, dear soul of my heart, that I am working so lovingly with you at this time. All of heaven awaits your plea for help so do look up to heaven, and ask these holy predecessors of yours to assist us in this holy process. Your mother is with you and will come to you as soon as you ask me. Great graces, my dear ones, have been set aside for God's consecrated souls so let us not waste even one. I extend my heavenly hands over you now as I place peace in your heart and courage in your soul. Jesus is pleased with your effort to work with your mother in this holy project. Do not disappoint Him. He longs to be united completely with you so that He can save the souls of his children. Remember that you are destined for this work, so the work is for you. Do not be afraid. We will proceed together in this endeavour and soon you will marvel at the graces bestowed upon you. That is all. Your mother blesses you. Be at peace. I am with you.

August 12, 2003
Blessed Mother

My children, my consecrated souls, how difficult these times have been for you. Do not think heaven has stood by idly while you have been so maligned and challenged in your faith. We are watching. We are giving strength. We are sustaining you and continue to do so while heaven organizes for the unity it is about to bestow upon the world. So now, little children, it is time for you to do your part. You have a role to play and it is important. Be assured that this plan from heaven is well thought out and you cannot improve upon it. So do not spend time talking about a better way, a different way, or your way. The plan I have outlined is to be completed only one way and that is heaven's way. Be docile receptacles of the great graces that gush from heaven now, directly into your heart. Be supportive of each other while we work through you. It is your task to begin this rescue mission and there are many souls who have been placed under your care. You will want every soul to be saved and will grieve at the loss of even one soul snatched by the darkness. You will be the light. You will reflect Christ and your followers will see Christ in you. How grateful you will be to have participated in the implementation of this plan. Many saints in heaven stand by, ready to be of service to you. Many angels arrange them-

selves around you in protection, awaiting your beckoning. Truly, you walk with the authority of Jesus Christ and must wear that authority with dignity and a firm purpose. It is not time for superfluous activity. It is time for deep prayer and commitment and the setting of a holy example, to both your fellow religious, and to the people who watch you for direction. Dear souls, be immovable in your stand on sin. Sin is an offence against the Godhead. Do every one of your followers know this? Have you told them this? If you have not, you will want to do so. You do not want people to be in the state of sin through ignorance, dear ones, as that is not fair to them. You are working against a dark world, that seeks to dismiss goodness as foolishness. Well, let us all be foolish now, dear souls under my care. Let us be foolish for Christ and allow nothing to stand between us and our full surrender to Christ. I am with you and direct your footsteps. Allow your mother to do this. You will not regret surrendering to heaven and the souls saved by your example will sing your glories for eternity. Do you want this? Let this be your goal then and nothing will weaken your resolve. Your work will be easy, I assure you. It is time to work in unity with heaven and with all righteous souls on earth who are also participating in this great renewal. Let us count you as one of the chosen servants of Christ and we will be about the business of saving souls. I bless you dear ones. I will never leave you. Your mother secures all graces for you and will answer your prayers in a special way right now. Ask for infinite graces for souls and these graces will be yours. Are you beginning to see Our plan? Spend time in prayer and you will see it unfold before you. You will also see your part, clearly lit. Your mother thanks you. Jesus, who will never be out-done in generosity, will reward you handsomely, even while you remain on earth. How grateful you will be, dear ones, for having been given the opportunity to walk this walk of salvation with Us. Go in peace now, to do great things.

August 12, 2003
Blessed Mother

My dear consecrated souls, it is with great joy that I speak to you today. Your mother has obtained great graces for you and these graces will help to guide you in your mission of love. Be assured of my constant guidance. I am watching you closely, alert to any sign that you need my motherly intervention. Little ones, there is no room for error now in your presentation of God's church. We seek to unify this church in a way that is consistent with times past, as opposed to times present. My son, the Holy Father, has been the victim of all manner of disobedience and malice. He was prepared for that and has carried his cross with great kindness, humility, and forgiveness. Not all could have carried such a cross. But all will bear their share of my Son's passion, if they are willing. And all will bear witness to the redemptive merit in the cross. By suffering you will save souls. Who could say no to the suffering Christ? Gaze upon the innocent form of my beloved Son as He silently writhes in pain on His cross. He suffered without benefit of the heavenly vision. You will not be asked to do that, except on rare occasion. The heavenly vision is to be laid open for your gaze. Indeed, you will have no need to ask if Christ is calling you. You will know Christ is calling you. Truly, I say to you, beloved children of my heart, your Father in heaven sustains this world far longer than He would have, because of the Passion of His Son. The intercessory powers of Jesus have saved the world and now God is choosing the most benign form of cleansing. Thank Him for this mercy, which will save countless souls from perdition. Children, graces such as these are received due to many sources. Please know that some of your holy lives, lived with such beautiful abandon to God's will, have obtained many graces being used right now during this time of renewal. Praise God that you have been allowed to participate. There is no comparison to union with Christ and that is what you are about to experience, if you want it. You know that heaven does not coerce a soul. A soul is invited to holiness and then to a higher level of holiness again. Would you like to begin your ascent now with decision? You can move more swiftly than you can imagine if you will only decide for Christ with abandon. I am here little one. Truly it is I, your heavenly mother, who beckons to you now. Do not ignore this final call to holiness.

August 13, 2003
Blessed Mother

My dear consecrated souls, I speak with you today to bring you joy. I want to share God's joy with you so you will understand why your work is so important. Do not be discouraged when you see lukewarm souls. We will bring God's grace to them and they will light up as they come to know my Son. You must practice your faith in an active, everyday sense. Have faith in God throughout the everyday hardships, difficulties, and challenges to your vocation. If you see something in your life that is not consistent with your vocation, you must move away from this threat to the perfection of your soul. And remember, my dear ones, that the perfecting of your soul is your base mission. You must always be moving closer to the Risen Christ or you will begin to move away. There is no standing still in the spiritual life, as you well know. We want you to be examples, as you have always been, but in an even more pronounced way at this time. Be obedient to the hierarchy of the church. Our own followers have helped to set the tone of disobedience that sits over this world like so much sickening smog. Our renewal is the fresh wind that is to blow this away so that the light of heaven can once again reach her children, giving them the hope they so long for. Our children are no longer flourishing in this world. Any parent would seek to remove children if their very development were at risk. My dear consecrated souls, this is what we are doing. Only instead of removing children, we are changing the environment. You must assist with this problem. God is no longer allowing this chokehold of sin. It is very simple. He has said, Enough. As with every people and every time, you must come to know the love of your God so you will not have to meet the wrath of your God. This is nothing new to you, souls of my heart. You have heard all of this before. The new part is the vast amount of grace that God is pouring over this world to fuel this renewal. That is why you are going to see your efforts succeed like they have not succeeded in the past. The world is asleep and we seek to wake it from that sleep. I will answer all of your questions in the silence of your hearts. Are you meeting me there, dear children? Are you meeting with Jesus, who waits patiently to infuse your vocation with divine sparks of the most powerful sort? My children, come back to Us in an extraordinary way. Take the first steps and We will greet you and I will pull you into the Sacred Heart of my Son, a furnace, which burns with love for you. Think of that now, my children. His heart burns with love for you. How often do you spend time just looking for His eyes in your soul. Do that for your mother today. Sit quietly with the Saviour and let Him show you how much He loves you. Truly, you will begin to change. Everyone who reads these words needs to move closer to Christ. Truly, I am speaking to you, my little child. Close your eyes now and feel my presence. Let the process begin as I bring you closer to my Son. Sit silently now as your mother ministers to your poor battered soul.

August 13, 2003
Blessed Mother

My dear ones, be grateful for this opportunity to join Us in this mission of redemption. You are truly blessed that We have chosen to come to you in this way. It is through these messages that we hope to bring you back to a full union with heaven, so that your work and duties will be divine and sanctioned by the divinity of the Lord Jesus Christ. In this way you will increase your effectiveness one hundred fold and one hundred fold again. Truly, there is no limit to what We can do, so be certain that you are letting Us lead and direct you. Otherwise, your work will be limited to human proportions, which is not what We require right now. Our work must be miraculous in its powers to convert. Souls must be brought back into the fold. Children, our standards must be set higher. And then higher again. We have to get back to a point when any misuse of the Lord's name is offensive. We have to get back to a point where even the smallest of lies causes the conscience to send off warnings and will bring a soul to the confessional. Can you say that this is the standard now? I think not. But this is where We are heading. Souls must understand, once again, the damage that sin does to their union with God. Souls must understand that union with God is the greatest priority of their day and their life. If this is threatened, they must not only be aware of it, but seek to rectify the damage done by the sin and become reunited with their God. Can you say that it is this way today? Of course you cannot because it is not this way. The majority of Our children have fallen by the wayside of the path to heaven. I do not want the logic of modern psychiatry. I assure you, it does not ring true in heaven and your God is not a psychiatrist and will not judge according to indulgent, character destroying theories, so embraced by your world. God is omniscient. He sees right into the centre of the soul. If you work with souls according to the theories of the modern world, you do them a disservice. They will not be able to use these theories as a shield to hold off divine judgement. Better you say to a soul, follow the path of righteousness. In the event you have been wronged, look clearly at what happened. Be assured God is displeased with the wrong levied against you. It was not God's will that you be injured. But God will judge your offender. The offender will not escape divine justice and the offence will not remain hidden. There are no successful lies or deceits in heaven, my children. And God will heal even the most grievous of wounds and injuries. Believe this. If you do not believe this, dear souls, how on earth can you convey this gift of healing to others? You cannot. It would be impossible. So you must obtain this gift of faith before you can share it. To obtain it, you must spend time with Jesus. There is no other way.

You cannot give what you do not have. Many have sought God's help through His servants and come away empty. What grief this causes to heaven. But no longer. We are working now toward full union of God's servants with Jesus. You must put your house in order again, beginning now. Then we can begin the walk into the world to rescue others. You have unlimited help with this task and I give you courage and joy. Be at peace dear ones. Mother will see to everything.

August 13, 2003
Blessed Mother

Dear children, I am worried for your safety, as a mother worries for her children when they are misled. Children, you must understand that any compromise with your faith is dangerous to you, to say nothing of the accountability attached to your leading of other souls. You must not compromise with modern interpretations of your faith. Do not take this statement as a license to be disobedient to the hierarchy of the church. That also is not my intention. My intention is this. I want you to rededicate yourself to your church. I want you to be faithful to the Vicar of Christ on earth. I want you to be intolerant, and I use that word deliberately, of any disobedience to this Chair of Christ, this Seat of Wisdom. You will have to be courageous in the face of such disobedience. It will feel odd initially, but look back through history. You face nothing that many of our other servants did not confront. Disobedience has always been present, you might think. Yes, this is unfortunately true. But believe me when I tell you that never in the history of this world has disobedience gone to such a blatant, destructive level. It threatens your very existence at this time and without the divine interference of God himself, you would not have a world to argue in. So do not use my words to create more division. This will be working against the plan. Use my words to justify your rededication to the Holy Father and the hierarchy of the church. Unless you are called upon directly to bring about change in the church, follow the rules of this church and serve with joy. Only work on instituting change if you are acting under obedience to your superiors. Little ones, trust me to intervene when there is something that needs to be adjusted. Tell me of these things and you will see me act. Again I tell you, these times are blessed with extraordinary graces so practice trust and you will be rewarded in a distinct, tangible way. There is nothing to fear and the changes to occur are God's will and therefore good for humanity and the world. Practice, become comfortable with giving your problems over to Jesus and soon it will be second nature. Much of your stress will be removed because you have refused to enter into the distraction game. And it is a game, dear ones. A game that we do not want you diverted with. Follow Jesus in your life. He will lead you to great accomplishments. Each soul is designed to achieve wonderful things but most souls today are refusing these graces. Children, I lovingly call you, with tenderness and motherly concern, but again, and always, with hope.

August 13, 2003
Blessed Mother

My dear consecrated souls, are you listening to your mother? Are you letting my messages reshape your soul and your direction? Perhaps you are angry at your mother. Tell me, dear little wounded soul. You may tell me if you are unhappy. Only through communication can we get to the root of the trouble and heal your pain. I do not want any blockages between us. So you must be honest. If you have healing that must be done, look around now. I will send you a holy soul to assist you. You will know this soul and with the help of this comrade, you can discover the source of your pain and we can lance any wounds that continue to take you from your mother. My child, injustice exists in your world. But injustice is not allowed in heaven. There is only love and celebration. Let me tell you about heaven so that you know and understand the glory of your destination. Heaven is filled with souls who love God. These souls, all filled with joy, explore every facet of the Divine. There is great knowledge to be had and anything you want to learn, you can learn. Imagine exulting in the accomplishments of all of the saints, both those who are known to you and those who are known only to God. In heaven, your accomplishments will be celebrated. Your faults, your sins, do not make the journey and are not only forgotten, but incinerated. Can you imagine, dear ones? Do you begin to picture this? Let me continue. In heaven, there are vast spaces, filled with every bit of beauty ever created by God. If, on earth, you create something that is divinely inspired, and this is what we want from you, it will endure in heaven, to be admired and explored by your brothers and sisters. Your spiritual relationships will also follow you to heaven. Every memory of your sins will be erased because you could not enjoy heaven if you were constantly annoyed by the memory of your mistakes. This is a mercy of God Himself and a good illustrative example of the character of your God. Please consider that more. He is never spiteful, never vengeful, and never punishes to punish. God, your all loving Father, moves only for the benefit of you, His creatures, created in love and hope. Children, I say to you with love, let go of your pain. I will help you. Ask me, please, and allow me to wash away the past hurts inflicted upon you by troubled souls. I wish your wholeness, your wellness, your confidence. Your healing is here, in my hand. I extend my hand to you now and place it in your heart. Be with me, dear one. It is to you, I speak.

August 13, 2003
Blessed Mother

Dear souls, I speak to you from motherly concern but also from motherly hope. I wish to direct you now to the great light that has been lit for you as a guide in this Age of Disobedience. My children, your questions will be answered. It is the usual practice that soldiers in a battlefield are not always privileged with the full strategic picture of the war being waged. Soldiers cannot worry about the full picture at times because they must concentrate on the specific campaign for which they are responsible. So do not be like curious children, who want all manner of information, even though it may not be to their benefit or it may not improve their performance. Be docile and humble. Trust that God has your best interests at heart and that through you, He protects the interests of the souls under your care. Be watchful, for any opportunity to serve. Encourage others to adapt this same attitude of alert helpfulness to heaven. Do you think God would be pleased with a job that is half done? It will disappoint Him and I promise you, if you disappoint Him, you will be grieved. Your heart will be sorrowful and there is nothing worse, my children, than regret and sadness over opportunities lost. I have said that, and you have understood. So we begin today. God loves you right now, and God wishes you to concentrate on what you are to do for Him today. He has projects assigned for you that will rely on your special gifts. These gifts are to be used for the Coming of the Kingdom. You must not use these gifts for your personal gain but we do not begrudge you support if you are called on to support yourself. We have thought of everything and there is an answer for everything. If you have a situation that is unclear to you, and you wish heavenly guidance, you have only to ask. I urge you to bring divine counsel into every area of your life. As we sift through each area, we will weed out the earthly motivations and insert heavenly motivations. This process will move swiftly. The more committed you are to Christ, the more swiftly it can move. Afterwards, you will work so much more efficiently. You will be happier, more content, and souls will be attracted you because of your singular focus. My children, all earthly education and teachings pale in comparison to the infused knowledge with which we wish to visit you. So be confident that you will have the ability to do anything we ask of you. Do not fear. Fear is not from God and prevents many soldiers from successfully completing their missions. Cast away fear and let us enjoy peace instead. I am with you and bless you. I will never leave you and your concerns will be my concerns. Look to souls who are led by me and you will see the peace in their faces. This is what I have for you. Heed my call, now, children. The time for service is today.

August 13, 2003
Blessed Mother

My dear souls, dedicated to Jesus, I wish to teach you more about goodness. Goodness comes from God. All goodness is rooted in heaven and blooms on earth. Your world is filled with a false goodness, that is really malice, disguised. Your world speaks of choice and lauds the choice of the individual. Well, this is fine, if a soul is choosing God. But to choose against the natural order, set down by God, is to bring the wrath of God down upon the world. These people are not working for goodness and their motives are not good. So do not feel compelled to pay homage to the modern concept of good any longer. Instead, ask the Holy Spirit to help you identify true goodness, the kind that is rooted in heaven, and the Spirit will direct you to examples. This same Spirit of Truth, will uncover the dark motives and malice of those who talk about good and work for bad. Now, do not be confused or concerned. When you see these individuals spouting their lies, you have felt confusion and a suspicion. It is that suspicion I wish to direct your attention to. Pay attention to those feelings and trust a little bit more in your holy instincts. Look at the fruits of various campaigns. Does a certain approach bear good fruit? And by that I mean does it bring souls into a unity with each other and with the Creator? You are not secular, dear ones. Please do not try to be. And do not be ashamed of your heavenly focus. If you are, you are ineffective to Us. Wear your faith as the badge of honour that it is. You work for Truth. You cannot work for Truth and be ashamed of Truth. This will never work. You must shout Truth from the rooftops now and stand firmly behind It. I will show you how. I am not looking for anything that is either beyond your reach or outside your capabilities. But I promise you, if you let Us work in you, you will see accomplishments you never dreamed would be associated with yourself. This is a time for great confidence. This is a time for great faith. And this is a time when great trust is necessary. Ask for these graces and these graces will be yours. Do you again see the trend? This is a trend away from the superficial tenets of your world and a trend toward the one Truth. The Truth is God. Nothing can substitute and nothing else will satisfy. So do not waste your time and please, do not waste your vocation on substitutions that do not satisfy. We are with you and intend to guide you with great specificity. Be blessed now, by both your mother and by my Son. It is through Him you will advance in your vocation. Learn from Him and emulate Him. Get to know Him. Remember to sit with Him in silence so that He can transfer His wisdom to you. Remember to ask Jesus to put love and devotion in your heart. He is with you always and seeks to place you in His heart. I extend my hands over you now in a motherly blessing. You are changing already, my child. Be joyful.

August 13, 2003
Blessed Mother

My dear ones, how happy I am to see you growing in love for your Creator. I wish to introduce you again to God, your Father. Your heavenly Father is all goodness. You can begin to understand Him if you look at the very best father on earth. He anticipates the needs of His children and has planned for every one of these needs. He has allowed mankind to advance in a remarkable fashion. This was intended for goodness, but alas, certain elements of mankind have twisted scientific discovery for evil purposes. Such evil is not tolerable to our Father because it is harmful to mankind, His finest creation. Think of the very best father on earth. How would you like this man's children to behave? Should they be obedient? Do they have any reason to rebel and be fearful? Should they eat one meal and then wail and moan because they fear they will not be given the next? How silly you would think them. How sad you would feel, to see children repaying such a loving and responsible father in that manner. Would you not reprimand those children? Would you not seek to correct them? Particularly if you had a large view and could see that every eventuality had been seen to and provided for. That is what I do, dear children. United with Christ, I seek to correct your world before it is destroyed by souls of malice. The

91

power of Christ is unlimited. It is unfathomable. It can do anything. It is so powerful that it is restrained. Christ is putting great faith in you, His followers, to prepare His children for His return. I do not seek to spread alarm and I tell you solemnly that if alarm is being spread, it is not being spread by people acting on my behalf. A mother never does that to her children. But she does caution them and provide them with every possible tool they need to do a job that she is asking them to do. I wish to lead you in this time and I have been given the authority to do so. Be docile to me. I ask you to be suspicious of those who spread error, but do not be suspicious of your mother. Look to the good fruits that arise from contact with me and truly, you will see, I am the woman clothed with the sun. I come to convince my children to work for the light and to embrace Jesus, who seeks only your salvation. I am here, dear one, watching over you. I pray for you and ask God to protect you every day. I cannot interfere though, if you march toward the wrong direction. I can only implore you to turn around and let me correct any error in your life. Look for peace and there you will see Christ. My authentic messages bring joy, peace, and enthusiasm, as opposed to fear, excitability, and division. So there is your test. Ask the Spirit to be with you and the Spirit will guide you. That is all for now. You must take these messages to your heart and let them blossom into a vocation of heavenly proportions. We are with you and applaud your smallest effort to turn toward heaven. Take those steps now, dear one, and see how those steps are rewarded and brought to greater steps. Once we are moving in the right direction, there will be no stopping the progress of your vocation. All of heaven is watching, encouraging, and waiting to help you. Look up to your friends, little one, and ask for their help. They await the opportunity to use the graces available to them so do not disappoint these heavenly souls, who want only to assist you. Do you see the glory of God's plan? We are all working together, heaven, earth, the Trinity, the angels, even the souls suffering in purgatory beseech heaven for great graces for you. God's majesty is unparalleled but you can begin to see glimpses of it now if you look. You may be excused for walking in delight, my child, as that is what we do in heaven.

August 13, 2003
Blessed Mother

Dear children, we must explore the Passion of Jesus. I want you to spend some time every day with Jesus in His passion. We have told you many things about this suffering and through the times we have revealed more and more. We do this to encourage your understanding of the great import of this heroic and merciful act. Jesus chose to die. He agreed to suffer. He acknowledged and accepted the dominion of sin over His mortal body and His limited time on earth. He did this with knowledge, it is true, and often you lack that knowledge, but you are called to trust, my little ones. You must trust that We have a redemptive plan for suffering that those on earth can not always understand. Suffering on earth has a place in the divine order of things. You will never create a world where those in the human body are free of all suffering. It is not ordained and is not going to happen. The only place you will be guaranteed no suffering is in heaven. Look closely at the value of suffering. Scrutinize those around you. Many have accepted suffering in their lives. They are neither bitter nor abandoned. Many have achieved great holiness. You often hear it said that if you want to talk to someone with character, talk to someone who has suffered. Those who do not accept suffering cannot even understand others, not to

95

mind minister to them and empathize. I do not want you to seek out suffering. That is not the point. I do want you to accept it lovingly and peacefully when it comes to your life. Please spend time with my Son in His passion. He looks down upon you with such love as you reflect on His passion. He is so consoled by your consideration of His pains and torment. Children, you would not leave your best friend to face that type of torture alone. You would not be a good friend if you did. Do not leave my Son to suffer alone. Walk with Him. Follow the Way of the Cross in silent consideration and let Him educate you on the merit of suffering. The Way of the Cross will come alive for you and you will never doubt the redemptive nature and value of suffering. Jesus, your Saviour, your dearest friend, seeks to reveal Himself to you now. He can only do that if you make yourself available to Him. Imagine a conversation where one party is turned away, busy with another task. The person attempting to communicate rightly gives up because there is nobody listening. Be certain, again I say, be certain, that this does not describe your relationship with Jesus. What has He said to you today? If He has said nothing, you are not listening. Turn to Him again now, and sit in silence, while he speaks to your heart. Close your eyes and see the loving smile on His face as He seeks to heal you and cleanse you. Your Jesus has many things to tell you, dear soul. You may cry to him, all of your pain, and He will take it away, to be replaced by joy. How happy and blessed I am to be the mother of this divine, gentle creature. How often has He consoled and enlightened me. I tell you children, if you are in communication with Jesus, there are no questions to be asked. So follow me, your heavenly mother, and I will see that you are united to Christ.

August 13, 2003
Blessed Mother

Dear consecrated souls, it is with great hope I come to you. I want you to consider the mercy of God, giving me this opportunity to bring you all of this guidance and love. I am teaching you about love, you see, as love is the mainstay and point of all that is relevant. All work must be centered in love. We have talked in the past about the modern version of love, which is not love at all, but exploitation. True love, heavenly love, is genuine. You know it is genuine because it creates security. Consider those with whom you are comfortable. Do you not see that those souls carry true love within them? It is safe to be with them because they carry a seed of God in them and that is what generates that love. It is that seed you respond to when you feel comfortable and safe with a person. Well, dear ones, I have to tell you that fewer and fewer carry that seed of love and that is why so many of your fellow brothers and sisters have fallen pray to diseases of the mind. Man was not meant to live without love in his life. He should walk through each day and experience a little love in this person, that person, and ideally, through every soul who has contact with him. But the Light has been extinguished in many souls and they have nothing to give in the way of love. Gradually, love in this man goes out too. Now a man can survive quite

99

nicely if he is nurtured by divine love. That is not a problem. But few souls are accepting divine love. Think on most of the souls you know. How many can you say have a lively connection to Jesus Christ? You will know them because they stand out. Why do they stand out? Because, they are joyful. They smile. They love others with simplicity and easiness. They worry for each other and tolerate and understand the faults of others. They seek to help others whenever they can. They are not ruled by addictions and jealousies. They do not acquire goods for the sake of acquiring goods. They speak the truth. They accept responsibility for their actions. And they like and respect children. How many souls of this description did you identify, dear one? I leave you with that thought and ask you to understand that this description should fit every one.

August 13, 2003
Blessed Mother

My dear children, you are accepting grace in your lives and that pleases me. My Son, also, draws great consolation from those souls who are responding to my promptings. Children, I know it is difficult for you at times. Remember that I lived the earthly life and drew much comfort from faith. I was often unsure of what the future held for my Son but I knew it was suffering. I lived with that reality, despite which I remained cheerful, dutiful, and joyful. You may ask how I did that. I tell you that I did it through prayer. I constantly asked our Heavenly Father to sustain me. When I felt the grief of my Son's future, I stopped whatever I was doing, and made an act of obedience to our Father. This became my life habit and it served me well, even during the most difficult hours. You will find this too. Whenever you feel unsure of yourself or afraid, make an act of obedience. Say the following: "God in heaven, I pledge my allegiance to you. I give you my life, my work, and my heart. In turn, give me the grace of obeying your every direction to the fullest possible extent." That is all children. That simple prayer will draw consolation down to you, consolation which will steady you and prepare you to proceed in His will. We do not judge you for your mistakes. We do not criticize. We want to guide you and if you turn the wrong way, we will simply correct you. Do not be afraid of failure, because, with God, failure is not possible. It is not even a possibility. Step forward now with joy, enriched by my words. Jesus, your Saviour, also has much to say to you, and will continue this heavenly direction. My children, humility is your watchword and love is your compass. You are being placed under my mantle of protection. Be assured of my constant, diligent, protection. None dare touch a child of this heavenly mother. Believe in this plan, children entrusted to me, and know that nothing will stop it. Indeed, it is progressing as we speak. God looks down upon you and sees a willing servant. You will spend eternity thanking Him for this opportunity to serve.

This book is part of a non-profit mission.
Our Lord has requested that we
spread these words internationally.

Please help us.

If you would like to participate,
please contact us at:

Direction for Our Times
12560 Holiday Drive
Alsip, Illinois 60803

708-385-7755

Anne does not benefit from the sale of these Volumes.

Jesus gives Anne a message for the
world on the first of each month.
To receive the monthly messages
you may access our website at
www.directionforourtimes.com
or call us at 708-385-7755
to be placed on our mailing list.

This book is from the series *Direction for Our Times as given to "Anne," A Lay Apostle*. Other volumes in this series are available from Direction for Our Times and are listed below:

A selection of tapes, DVD's and CD's featuring interviews with Anne, Archbishop Hannan and Mary Lou McCall are available through Focus Worldwide Network. These initial interviews were filmed in October 2004. They offer stirring insight and reflections on the messages of Direction for Our Times.

Please contact Focus Worldwide Network to purchase copies.

Focus Worldwide Network
106 Metairie Lawn Drive
Metairie, LA 70001

Phone: 504-840-9898
Fax: 504-840-9818
www.focusvideos.com

Copies of these video tapes may also be purchased from Direction for Our Times at 1-708-385-7755.